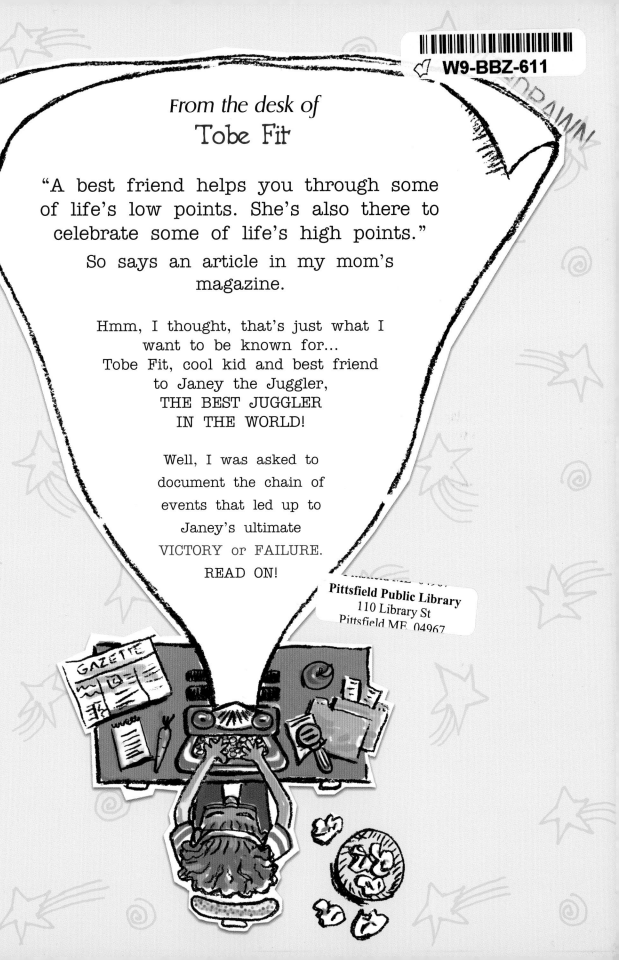

From the desk of
Tobe Fit

"A best friend helps you through some of life's low points. She's also there to celebrate some of life's high points."

So says an article in my mom's magazine.

Hmm, I thought, that's just what I want to be known for...
Tobe Fit, cool kid and best friend to Janey the Juggler,
THE BEST JUGGLER
IN THE WORLD!

Well, I was asked to document the chain of events that led up to Janey's ultimate
VICTORY or FAILURE.
READ ON!

Acknowledgements

Thanks to the millions of school children, parents, and teachers throughout the country
to whom we've have had the privilege of presenting our live FOODPLAY shows –
it is you who have helped bring Tobe and Janey to life!

The creative support and contribution of Fran Schneid in making this book a reality is acknowledged with deep appreciation. Thanks to Lee Newton for assistance in art direction and George Foster and Michael Nelson for book design expertise. Thanks to all those who reviewed and/or field-tested this book, especially Anna Kirwan, Dori Ostermiller, Tobi Sznajderman, Jesse Harris, Lily Harris, Patricia Messing, Michelle Nicole Wesley, Margo Wootan, Jeanine Laborne, Caren Epstein, Molly Tarleton, Marilyn Toth, Bill Pohl, Cindy Coughlin, the Mattahunt, Beal and Hatfield Elementary Schools, and all the folks at FoodPlay Productions - Melinda Beasi, Cori Hanrahan, Lauren Marciszyn, Elissa Thornton, Staysee Bogan, Ann Marie Rex, Jewelia Rex, Meloney Delisle, Patti Dougherty, Megan Cannon, Adam Oliveri, and Jason Westbrook. And, thanks to my family and friends, especially Natalie, David, Dan, and Amy Storper; Sarah, Gerry, Aaron, and Jessica Field; Muriel, Bob, and Kevin Goldfarb; Helena Reynolds, and Rita Ranan - who support me in my mission.
– BFS

To my husband, Joel, for his generosity and unwavering support of my work on this project.
And to my daughters, Dan and Sam, for showing me that being a mother is the most important job in the world!
– FES

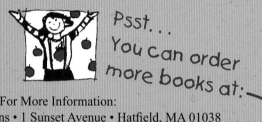

Psst... You can order more books at:

For More Information:
FoodPlay Productions • 1 Sunset Avenue • Hatfield, MA 01038
1-800-FOODPLAY • info@foodplay.com • www.foodplay.com

Publisher's Cataloging-in-Publication Data

Storper, Barbara Faith.
Janey Junkfood's fresh adventure! : making good eating great fun! /
by Barbara F. Storper, MS, RD ; illustrated by Frances E. Schneid.
   p. cm.
   ISBN 978-0-9642858-5-9
Summary: Tobe makes good eating great fun to help her best
friend, Janey, get off the junk food track in order to make the
Junior National Juggling Team. Includes 14 fun snack recipe cards.

[1. Children--Nutrition–Fiction. 2. Food habits–Fiction. 3. Food–
Fiction. 4. Cookery–Fiction. 5. Diet–Fiction. 6. Health behavior–
Fiction.] I. Schneid, Frances. II. Title.
PZ8.3.S8745 Ja 2007   [E]–dc22   2007924586

Written by: Barbara Storper, MS, RD
Creative/Art Director: Barbara Storper, MS, RD
Design, Layout, and Illustrations: Frances E. Schneid
Graphic Art Consultant: Lee Newton
Production Coordination: Jennifer Goodheart
Front Cover Design: Frances E. Schneid
Back Cover Design: George Foster

Janey Junkfood's
Fresh Adventure!

By Tobe Fit

With a little
help from:

Barbara Storper, MS, RD (words)

and Frances E. Schneid (pictures)

FOODPLAY productions

FoodPlay Preliminary Edition

My Dedication

This book is dedicated to my mother,
who taught me how TO BE the best I can be.
It's also dedicated to Mother Nature,
for making us so many great foods to eat –
foods that are good for our health
and good for the health of the planet, too!

Thanks, Moms!

-TF

Hi!

My name is Tobe, Tobe Fit.
Pronounced:

TOE   BEE   FIT   ME

I know what you may be thinking . . . that Tobe's a dog's name. Well, that may be true some of the time. According to my research, there are more dogs named:

Tobey Tobi Toby

than any other name.

Of course, they don't spell it the same way as me! And, besides, I love dogs, so I don't mind sharing the fame of my name with them.

ANYWAY,
enough about me! This story's really about my best friend

↓   ↓   ↓

JANEY

Dalmatian, Tobi, Receives Award

Tobi, receives award from Fire Marshal, for outstanding service to his community.

Tobi has been with Fire House No. 5 for ten years. He has saved many lives from children to adults. Today he is being honored for his heroism and his community.

BEST SHOW DOG TOBY

Janey and I have LOTS in common . . .   1

Stuff We Have In COMMON:

1. We both live with just one of our parents. ♡ ♡

2. We both have ANNOYING little brothers.

3. And last, but most important of all, we both want to GET OUT of our hometown, Springfield, and

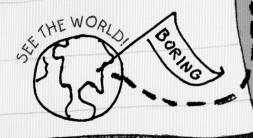
SEE THE WORLD! BORING

BUT...

There's also stuff we don't have in common.

That's OK, too, because my Mom's article on friendship says that best friends can be as different from each other as DAY and NIGHT,

Vanilla and Chocolate,

Apples and Oranges!

As for me, I want to be a

DETECTIVE

when I grow up –

you know, investigate stuff, dig for dirt, get to the bottom of things. And, Janey, well, she wants to be, GET THIS –

See, Janey LOVES to JUGGLE. And, I don't mean just being able to catch a piece of popcorn in her mouth, the way my little brother, Willie, is always trying to do at the WORST times (like, when I'm trying to

CONCENTRATE

on a difficult detective case).

I mean Janey can REALLY juggle!

In fact, Janey's ALWAYS trying to juggle SOMETHING(s)!

Here's Janey juggling her shoes and socks!

And, at school, she'll juggle everyone's lunches in the middle of the cafeteria!

That makes her really popular with the kids, but the lunch ladies are not very happy!

"JANEY Don't PLAY with Your FOOD!"

But she keeps juggling away.

Well, that brings me
to this story...

Me
Janey

One day, Janey came to me with this

BRIGHT   IDEA

"I know how we can get to ~~travil~~ travel around the world," she said. Then, she showed me this picture from a magazine.

Janey
Me

"Tobe, did you know there's a Junior National Juggling Team? The kids are so good that they get to juggle in contests all over the world." She figured, if she could get REALLY GOOD, she could make the Nationals, and then she could travel around the world, too!

JUGGLE

THE NJJ TEAM

TRAVEL

MAP of EUROPE

Tobe

Janey

"And just M A Y B E," she said, "you could come along to cheer me on!"

"SWEET idea," I said.

PASSPORT

So, Janey started to practice really hard.

She practiced with ⚫⚫ BALLS

then ⚫⚫⚫ then ⚫⚫⚫

then ⚫⚫

then ⚫

She figured she'd need to come up with the most incredible juggling routine to impress the judges.

HER PLAN:

1. Juggle five balls in the air

2. Balance a loaf of French bread on her nose*

3. All while riding on top of a six foot unicycle (a bicycle with only one wheel)!

* She thought adding a French bread might make her seem very I N T E R N A T I O N A L and improve her chances with the judges!

Things, however, were NOT going as well as planned.

1.

2.

3.

JANEY was finally able to climb up onto a three foot unicycle.

She got as far as putting a HOT DOG BUN on her nose (which always fell off) and then her dog,

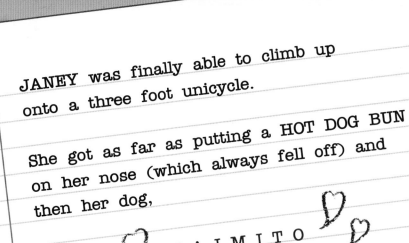

JAIMITO

(pronounced Hi - Me - Toe)

would run over and start to EAT IT and then spit it out in little drool-covered spit balls.

As for the REST, she kept DROPPING the BALLS!!

No one at her juggling club knew what to do or how to help.

So, being that I'm going to be a detective when I grow up, I figured I'd need to investigate the situation, you know, examine the evidence, find out why Janey keeps messing up.

The very next day

Take a CLOSER LOOK at 8:15 am

AHA! THE EVIDENCE:

Sugary JUNK FOOD instead of a good, nutritious BREAKFAST!

No wonder she crashed. If there's one thing my mom always tells me it's

SUGAR ENERGY DOESN'T LAST!

Inside
The ^SCOOP on SUGAR

By Food Detective, Tobe Fit

SODA

10 teaspoons of SUGAR!

APPLE PIE

+ 11 teaspoons of SUGAR!

CAUTION

A TOTAL of 21 TEASPOONS of SUGAR! Ugh!

Then it came to me —
The NUMBER ONE THING Janey and I never had in COMMON.
Can you guess what it is?
(Clue: look closely at the photos in my scrapbook.)

JJ
~~JANEY~~ and ME

Janey and me
at Beach Pre-K

Janey and me at
the 3rd grade picnic

ANSWER:
Junk food

Janey and "friend" on
her 9th Birthday

Ever since I can remember,
Janey's been on the
"SEAFOOD" Diet —
She eats all the
JUNK FOOD
she SEES!!!

Ha! Ha! Ha! Get it?

I know, I'll call her JJ,
short for "Janey Junkfood".
She'll think it stands for
"Janey the Juggler,"
so nobody will get mad!

I proceeded to do some background research:

Hoop Hero Takes a Stand on Breakfast

University of Connecticut basketball star Michelle Gordon visited the Hennigan Middle School in Cleveland, Ohio yesterday for an afternoon assembly amidst crowds of enthusiastic fans. When asked, "What's the best thing you

TODAY'S SPORTS

can do if you want to be a winner?" she replied confidently, "eat a good breakfast – you need to gas up your engine with premium fuel and that's the truth!"

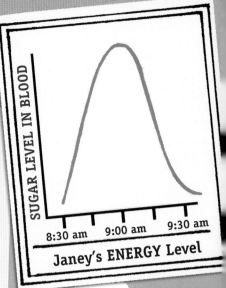

Janey's ENERGY Level

BONKS OUT ON SUGAR!

World renowned cyclist, Vance Legstrong, # 1 rated American cyclist, ruined his chances to win his 6th Tour De Paris, by one morning's poor choice of breakfast! According to Legstrong, he woke up late, didn't have time for his usual oatmeal, orange juice, egg and toast, and instead, grabbed a candy bar. The sugar gave him a quick spurt of energy, but not the kind that lasts. He couldn't even make it up his first hill, and had to leave the race in search of a good breakfast. He blames it all on the sweet stuff. "Never again," he exclaimed, "never again!"

American Youth Eat More than their Weight in SUGAR!

It's official! The average American child eats over 150 pounds of sugar a year – that's more than most kids weigh! Two hundred years ago, the average child ate only two pounds of sugar a year.

In the last twenty years, obesity rates have doubled among children and tripled among teenagers.

Tooth decay has skyrocketed and "adult-onset" diabetes, once considered a disease which only affected adults, is now occurring in children at record numbers. One out of every three children in the U.S. is expected to get diabetes in his or her lifetime if today's eating and exercise habits don't improve.

SUGAR FILES

THE CASE AGAINST JUNK FOOD

An interview with a famous nutritionist (my mom) as transcribed by yours truly, Tobe Fit.

ME: So, what exactly is wrong with junk food anyway?

FAMOUS NUTRITIONIST:

1 Well for starters, junk food doesn't give you the kind of energy that lasts, so you quickly tire out! Then you reach for more, to get you going again. It's up and down, up and down — you're treating your body like a yo-yo!

2 Junk food doesn't give your body the nutrients it needs to grow, get strong, or keep you from getting sick.

3 Junk food is full of sugar, fat, and salt that stress out your organs, especially your heart, and weaken all your body's systems.

4 Junk food is full of artificial ingredients that trick your body into craving more, so you just can't
S - T - O - P !

5 Finally, junk food is full of empty calories that just fill you up and OUT!

Remember — it's ok to eat junk food once in a while, as long as you mostly feed your body wholesome foods and have fun being active!

It's all about BALANCE!

Janey's on a sugar roller coaster and she can't get off!

Sugar Crash

"Tobe! YOU'RE NUTS! Get rid of my Junkfood? NO WAY You CAN'T take my JUNKFOOD away!"

Oh, well, I thought, another missed opportunity at greatness.

I guess we'll be stuck here in Springfield for the rest of our lives only dreaming of fame, travel, and fortune.

What a ROYAL DRAG!

Then my Opportunity of a Lifetime savers came

Detective Log

Tuesday, 9 o'clock a.m.

Hmm, 3 weeks? Aargh! Uh oh, Janey really needs me now. She'll never make the team with those junky eating habits!

But, what can I do?

How can I, Tobe Fit, change the course of human events? Right the wrongs of history? Discover the cure for . . .

Oh, wait a second, I'm getting carried away.

Tobe,
What can I do? TRY-OUTS are only 3 weeks away! H-E-L-P Me PLEASE!!! JJ

NJJT

NATIONAL JUNIOR JUGGLING TEAM

TRY-OUTS!

Jackson Middle School Gym
Wednesday, May 21st
7 P.M.

Join the National Junior Juggling Team! Represent your country while you JUGGLE your way around the WORLD!

• Only SERIOUS JUGGLERS need apply •

Tuesday, 6:32 p.m.

I know, if I could just show Janey the evidence--what's in all the junk food she keeps eating and what it's doing to her body — then, maybe she'd change her junky habits.

Yeah, that just might work.

On to Plan A—

Janey's snacks:

UNCOVERED

15

JANEY, LOOK WHAT'S IN YOUR APPLE PIE!

Use my top secret label decoder to decode the hidden sugars, fats, and additives. **Read It Before You Eat It!**

Label Decoder

Red Words = Sugars
Blue Words = Fats
Brown Words = Additives
Green Words = Good Stuff

APPLE PIE $1⁰⁰

INGREDIENTS: Flour, sulfite-treated apples, partially hydrogenated vegetable oil and/or animal shortening, high fructose corn syrup, corn syrup, sugar, water, brown sugar, modified corn starch, soy flour, salt, whey, soy protein isolate, calcium and sodium caseinate, calcium carbonate, calcium sulfate, agar, locust bean gum, dextrose, sodium phosphate, corn flour, corn dextrin, cinnamon, nutmeg, citric acid, cornstarch, lemon juice solids, lemon oil, potassium citrate, sorbitol, tricalcium phosphate, artificial flavor, sodium propionate, sorbic acid, RD&C Yellow 5, Red 40.

Yeech! The only good things in there are "THEM APPLES!"

And, Janey, you could've eaten:

1 2 3 4 5 6 7 fresh apples for the same calories or

1 2 3 fresh apples for the same price as one measly pie! **RAW DEAL!**

AND LOOK WHAT'S IN YOUR SODA!!

10 teaspoons — Sugar ① — water — Caffeine ② — Phosphoric Acid ③ — Colorings ④ — Flavorings ⑤

KEY TO INGREDIENTS

1. **Sugar:**
   Ten teaspoons a CAN— that's *160 empty calories* from **SUGAR!**

2. **Caffeine:**
   A drug that stimulates your central nervous system, making you wired, then tired. The caffeine in a can of soda affects kids twice as much as adults, due to our smaller body size.

3. **Phosphoric Acid:**
   Eats away tooth enamel, leading to cavities. Also, can cause calcium to be leeched from bones.

4. **Colorings:**
   To make it look dark.

5. **Flavorings:**
   Top secret formula!

Tooth soaked in COLA for 24 hours.

Broken bone of teenager who drank too much SODA.

JJ--Here's what could happen if you don't treat your body right!
Anatomy of A
junkfood diet!
HAIR LOSS
CRANKY
BAD BREATH AND ROTTEN TEETH
PIMPLY SKIN
WEAK MUSCLES
HEART DISEASE AND DIABETES
OVERWEIGHT
HOLEY BONES
POOR DIGESTION AND CONSTIPATION
SORES
BOW LEGGED
Tobe—
That's gross!
But I love
the way
junk food
tastes!

Hmm...this was going to be harder than I thought. If I could just get Janey to try something healthy, I bet she'd end up liking it.

But, how could I get her to try her first bite???

The next day at Juggling Club . . .

HEY... WHAT HAPPENED TO MY JUGGLING BALLS?

WHAT ARE THESE DOING HERE?

C'MON JANEY, YOU'RE LATE AGAIN... GET ON THE BALL.

BUT, BUT, COACH...

HEY EVERYBODY, LOOK, JANEY'S GONNA JUGGLE SOME FRUIT! HEY MAYBE SHE'LL EVEN TAKE A BITE!

JANEY'S GOING TO EAT THE APPLE AS SHE JUGGLES THE APPLE! NO WAY! THIS WE GOTTA SEE!

BUT WHAT COULD SHE DO? ALL EYES WERE ON HER.

I WILL NOW ATTEMPT TO DO THE IMPOSSIBLE, EAT THE APPLE AT THE SAME TIME AS I JUGGLE THE APPLE.

JANEY, YOU CAN DO IT!

OH, WHY ME? OK, WELL, ER, HERE I GO.

LITTLE DID EVERYONE KNOW HOW HARD THIS REALLY WOULD BE FOR JJ.

YUCK, THAT'S NOT THE APPLE!

THAT'S AN ORANGE!

THIS IS THE APPLE!

IT'S THE RED ONE!

(CHOMP) YUM (CHOMP) SWEET.... (CHOMP, CHOMP) JUICY.... BOY THIS APPLE SURE IS GOOD!

YAY FOR JANEY! COOL TRICK!

YOU DID IT — YOU REALLY DID IT.

YEAH TOBE, I DID IT! HEY, WAIT A SECOND. IT WAS YOU— YOU SWITCHED MY JUGGLING BALLS!

WINK, WINK!

...AND EVERYBODY LIVED HAPPILY AND HEALTHFULLY EVER AFTER — OR, SO I WISHED!

WELL I GUESS APPLES ARE OK ONCE IN A WHILE.

BUT YOU DON'T EXPECT ME JUST TO EAT APPLES, DO YOU?

WHAT ELSE IS THERE?

WHAT ELSE IS THERE ???

Then, all the kids in juggling club started shouting out their favorite snacks...

But, she'll need help —
a little help from her friends!

That's when I got my BEST idea yet!
We can make her tickets —

TICKETS to ✶ FRESH ✶ ADVENTURES!

(Each one is good for one nutritious and delicious snack!)

Every time Janey gives us a ticket,
we'll make her one of our favorite
snacks together. That way, she
doesn't have to buy junk food
at the store!

TIX 4 U!!!
→
go 2 end of book

Yogurt Parfait
Ticket to FRESH Adventures!

Veggie Grab Bag
Ticket to FRESH Adventures!

ace
Ticket to FRESH Adventures!

EAT TO WIN!

Less than 3 weeks to tryouts!

3 weeks later

MAY 21 — Veggie Confetti ☺

MAY 2 — Apple Smiles ☺

MAY 18 — Natural Soda ☺

MAY 16 — Yogurt Parfait ☺

MAY 14 — Veggie Robot ☺

MAY 17 — Chili Sticks

Did Janey get off the junk food track?

Did she become a STAR JUGGLER?

WILL SHE MAKE THE TEAM?

Hey Look, tickets to Janey's TRYOUTS!

TICKET

TICKET

TICKET

Dear Tobe,

Here are YOUR tickets — tickets to my tryouts. Make sure everyone from juggling club comes and pay careful attention to my

"NEW AND IMPROVED" Juggling Routine.

Cross your fingers and wish me (lots of) luck!

Faithfully yours,
Janey

P.S. Thanks for being the BESTEST friend ever!

22

THE MOMENT of Truth!

Evening of May 21st:

The gym is packed with people. There are so many kids waiting to try out, and they all look so much older. Not only that, Janey's second to last in line!

Uh oh, these kids sure can juggle!

Finally it's Janey's turn.

She comes out, nervous and shaking. She moves slowly toward the center of the stage. She looks out into the audience, then at the judges, then her eyes finally find me in the front row.

We look at each other, we both take a deep breath, and I give her a

HIGH 5!

"You can do it, Janey!" And she begins.

Poor Janey, This is going to be TOUGH!

But, wait — LOOK!!!

What's that in her hands? Instead of juggling balls, she has -

"My name is Janey and I'm feeling good,

I love to juggle in my neighborhood.
My best friend, Tobe, she's real cool,
she taught me all about the 'Eat-to-Win' Rule.

To keep your body
healthy and strong,
feed it primo fuel
and you can't go wrong.

Try something new,
fresh and nutritious,
it doesn't have to be
junk food to be delicious!

Veggie confetti and yogurt parfait,
crunchy baby carrots,
fantastic fruits from far away.
Juicy watermelon and luscious papaya,
up they go, up they go,
higher and higher!

24

Look, I can throw 1-2-3-4-5 into the air,
an apple, banana, peach, plum, and a pear!
Don't blink for a second, you might miss my best trick,
taking a bite from the apple, it's my favorite snack pick.

'Amazing!' they say (chomp),
'Oh what a feat!' (chomp),
to eat (chomp) while I juggle
Mother Nature's sweet treats!

But, uh oh, my mouth is completely full,
and I need to remember my own mother's rule.
What does she tell me, to show I'm polite?
'Don't talk with your mouth full,
it's a terrible sight!'

So, now if you will,
I will end my routine,
and hope you choose me, JANEY,
to be on your team!"

WOW — Janey did GREAT!

But, then I turn to the judges.

They all look so serious —
there's not one smile on their faces.

They're busy writing stuff down and
whispering to each other.

Oh, what can this mean?

Poor Janey,
Poor Me!

Everything's going in slow motion.
A few seconds seem like a lifetime.

Finally, the judges raise
their score cards . . .

She did it! She did it!
She made the TEAM!!!

DAILY
GAZETTE

MAY 22

THURSDAY

SUNNY

LOCAL GIRL MAKES TEAM!

Scores Perfect "10" in Juggling Try-Outs

SPRINGFIELD GIRL MAKES NATIONAL JUNIOR JUGGLING TEAM!

Janey Juarez, a twelve-year-old student at Jackson Middle School, has just made the National Junior Juggling Team—a U.S. team of youngsters that tours around the world competing with jugglers from different countries.

Janey was considered to be a juggling prodigy when she was only seven years old, but seemed to have trouble in recent years performing tricks successfully. When asked, what was her new found secret to success, she smiled and said, "You have to eat to win!"

When questioned further, Janey replied, "I kept dropping the balls until I learned how to treat my body right! Now, I make sure to eat a good breakfast, eat lots of fresh fruits and vegetables, and quit eating so much junk food!"

Ja
su

Janey credits her success to her best friend, <u>Tobe Fit</u>, and their Fresh Fruit and Veggie Adventures!

And the front page of the newspaper!

Hey, look--So did I!

And then, dear reader, you'll never guess what happened.
Everyone on the team was so impressed with Janey's progress,
that they awarded me, Tobe Fit, the official title of
'ACE FOOD DETECTIVE'
for the National Junior Juggling Team.

And, guess what?
They want me to travel with them around the world to
help get all the members into shape for the upcoming
World Juggling Championships!

And, just to think, it all started because
Janey kept dropping the ball!

SPLAT!

Psst -- Your FRESH Adventure starts here

Yogurt Parfait

Ticket to FRESH Adventures!

Apple Smiles

Ticket to FRESH Adventures!

Party Platter for One

Ticket to FRESH Adventures!

Shake It UP Baby

Ticket to FRESH Adventures!

Natural Soda

Ticket to FRESH Adventures!

Chill Sticks

Ticket to FRESH Adventures!

Fantastic Fruits from Far Away

Ticket to FRESH Adventures!

FRESH Adventure! Snack Club

★ Official Membership Card ★

Welcome! Write your name here.

www.foodplaykids.com

★APPLE SMILES★

Make a sandwich with fruit as the bread! Wash and cut an **apple or pear** into thin wedges. Pat dry. Then, put a slice of **cheese** or spread **peanut butter** in between the two wedges. Squeeze gently. You can even smoosh **puffed rice cereal** into the peanut butter between the two slices for "teeth"! Smile as you eat it, and say "cheese"!

From Emma

Always have a grown-up with you to help!
★not recommended for kids under 5 - choking risk★

★YOGURT PARFAIT★

You'll need **yogurt, fresh fruit,** such as **strawberries** and **bananas**, and a pretty dish or clear cup. Put a layer of yogurt, then a layer of washed, cut-up fruit, then yogurt, then fruit, then yogurt. Top off with a **crunchy topping**: nuts, trail mix, dry cereal, crushed graham crackers, or granola. It's scrumptuliumptious!

Your friend, Terell

Always have a grown-up with you to help!
★not recommended for kids under 5 - choking risk★

★SHAKE IT UP, BABY!★

Smoothies are great for a snack or quick breakfast! Put into a blender, **fresh fruit** such as 1/2 a **banana** and 1/2 cup of washed **strawberries**. Add 1/2 cup of **yogurt** and 1/2 cup of **orange juice or milk**. Cover and blend till smooth and frothy. (To be extra prepared, you can freeze slices of super ripe **bananas** in plastic bags and use them in your smoothies!)

Bon Appétit, Shira

Always have a grown-up with you to help!

★PARTY PLATTER FOR ONE!★

I make this for my mom after a hard day of work but also for myself sometimes, as a special treat after school. Wash and cut up your favorite **fruits** into pieces. Also, cut up pieces of **cheese**. Arrange on a pretty platter with **crackers**. To be extra fancy, add toothpicks to the fruit and serve with a dip of **fruit-flavored yogurt.** Enjoy!

Love, Shantie

Always have a grown-up with you to help!
★not recommended for kids under 5 - choking risk★

★CHILL STIX★

In Mexico, we take a **papaya or mango**, peel off the skin and cut it into slices. Then, we put the slices onto a popsicle stick and squeeze a little **lime juice** on, and surprise, a fruit popsicle! You can also put other cut-up fruit on a popsicle stick, wrap in plastic, and freeze. My favorite "Chill Stix" have **strawberries** and **banana** slices. Chill out!

Your buddy, Maria

Always have a grown-up with you to help!
★not recommended for kids under 5 - choking risk★

★NATURAL SODA★

Here's an easy way to make soda, naturally! Fill up a glass halfway with your favorite **100% fruit juice**. Fill the rest of the glass with **bubbly water (seltzer)** and stir.

Give your soda a jazzy name –
I call mine "Orange Sizzler!"

Drink up! – Malik

Always have a grown-up with you to help!

FRESH Adventure! Score Card

| How'd ya like it? YUMMY☺ YUCKY☹ TRY AGAIN😐 |

- ○ Yogurt Parfait
- ○ Apple Smiles
- ○ Party Platter
- ○ Shake It Up, Baby!
- ○ Natural Soda
- ○ Chill Stix
- ○ Fantastic Fruits
- ○ Veggie Grab Bag
- ○ Sushi Rolls
- ○ Veggie Robots
- ○ Salsa Sticks
- ○ Make a Face!
- ○ Broccoli Forest
- ○ Veggie Confetti

★FANTASTIC FRUITS FROM FAR AWAY!★

Whenever you have the chance, be daring and try a far-out **fruit that you've never tried before**! My favorites – star fruit, pomegranate, and fresh figs! You can even investigate the far away places where the fruit comes from. Have a "tasting party" with your friends or in class, where each of you brings in an exotic fruit to share!

– Joshua wishes you the best!

Always have a grown-up with you to help!
★not recommended for kids under 5 - choking risk★

Ticket to FRESH Adventures!

Ticket to FRESH Adventures!

Ticket to FRESH Adventures!

Ticket to FRESH Adventures!

Ticket to FRESH Adventures!

Ticket to FRESH Adventures!

Ticket to FRESH Adventures!

Tobe Fit's EAT-to-WIN Tips

- ★ Fuel up with a nutritious breakfast!
- ★ Go fresh with fruits and veggies!
- ★ Eat a variety from all five food groups!
- ★ Read it before you eat it!
- ★ Feed your body healthy food and your mind, healthy messages!

www.foodplaykids.com

★ SUSHI ROLLS ★

If you can't make the real thing like my dad does, make these. You'll need: a **slice of bread**; **hummus or soft cheese** like ricotta or cream cheese; thin sticks of raw, washed **carrots**, **celery**, and/or **cucumber**; and **sprouts** (optional). First, flatten bread with hands or a roller. Then spread hummus or cheese on bread. Put veggies in center, roll up and eat! Kampai! (That means "Cheers!" in Japanese.) – From Tak

Always have a grown-up with you to help!
★ not recommended for kids under 5 - choking risk ★

★ VEGGIE GRAB BAG ★

A fun snack to pack and eat on the go! Wash and cut up crunchy **fresh veggies** that you have in the fridge, such as carrots, celery, green/red/yellow peppers, string beans, and jícama. Then, put them in a small plastic bag. Or, for a frozen treat in summertime, bag up frozen peas and eat 'em before they turn into mush!

Give Peas a Chance! Tafari

Always have a grown-up with you to help!
★ not recommended for kids under 5 - choking risk ★

★ SALSA STICKS ★

Put **cheese** (grated or sliced) on a **tortilla or flat bread.** Have a grown-up cook it in a toaster oven (cheese side facing up) or microwave until cheese melts. Then, carefully take it out and roll up. Dip into **salsa** - YUM! For homemade salsa, mix together cut-up ripe tomatoes, onions, cilantro, and celery. Add lime or lemon juice. Muy sabrosa! (That means "delicious" in Spanish.)

– Carlos

Always have a grown-up with you to help!
★ not recommended for kids under 5 - choking risk ★

★ VEGGIE ROBOTS ★

Take me to your leader! Have a grown-up help you wash and cut-up different **raw veggies** into various sizes and shapes. Then, create your own veggie robot by putting pieces together with **toothpicks**. When you're done, take your robot apart, piece by piece, and dip into **salad dressing** for a crunchy treat! Be extra careful with the toothpicks - don't poke yourself!

Your friend, Ángel

Always have a grown-up with you to help!
★ not recommended for kids under 5 - choking risk ★

★ BROCCOLI FOREST ★

Create your own "forest" by washing and cutting off little "trees" from a **broccoli** stalk. Make your "dirt" with this dip: combine 1/4 cup of **peanut butter**, 1 tablespoon of **cider vinegar**, 2 teaspoons of **soy sauce**, 1 teaspoon of **brown sugar**, and 5 tablespoons of **water**. Mix well. Add a splash of **cayenne pepper** or **hot sauce** to spice it up! Dunk your "trees" into "dirt" and enjoy!

Go Green! – Sophie

Always have a grown-up with you to help!
★ not recommended for kids under 5 - choking risk ★

★ MAKE A FACE! ★

You can use a **rice cake or piece of bread** (whole grain is best!) as the base of your masterpiece. Spread **peanut butter**, **almond butter**, **hummus**, **or soft cheese** on one side. Then, make a face - eyes, nose, mouth, and hair - with cut-up, washed **veggies** such as carrots, green peppers, sprouts, and olives. Eat up!

Olive you! – Olivia

Always have a grown-up with you to help!
★ not recommended for kids under 5 - choking risk ★

★ Quick & Easy Pyramid Power Snacks ★

★ popcorn • pretzels • rice cakes • graham crackers muffins • bagels • cereals • granola • sandwiches pasta • fig bars • veggies • baby carrots • edamame pickles • guacamole • salsa • veggie pizza • salad fruit • applesauce • raisins • dried fruit • string cheese pudding • yogurt • frozen yogurt • cheese + crackers trail mix • sunflower seeds • pumpkin seeds • almonds peanuts • hummus • leftovers • tacos • rice + beans • sushi 100% fruit juice • 100% veggie juice • low-fat milk water • flavored selters ★

Always have a grown-up with you to help!
★ not recommended for kids under 5 - choking risk ★

★ VEGGIE CONFETTI ★

Wash and cut up into small pieces crunchy **raw veggies** - green peppers, carrots, celery, jícama, and/or radishes - whatever you have in the fridge. Mix up in a bowl. If you want, drizzle on some salad dressing. Munch on this instead of popcorn as you watch your favorite movie!

Here's to you! – Keisha

Always have a grown-up with you to help!
★ not recommended for kids under 5 - choking risk ★

© 2007 FoodPlay Productions, LLC   www.foodplay.com

Greetings from

NATIONAL JUNIOR JUGGLING TEAM

Hey, Everyone —

We're having a ball, but I MISS YOU guys!
Traveling is fun, but there's no place
like home.

Remember - you don't have to travel
around the world to have a Fresh Adventure —
Just let your TASTE BUDS do the WALKING!

Happy Travels,
Janey the Juggler

To:
Jackson St. Juggling Club
Jackson Middle School
Springfield, USA 0X0X0

USA
&
be
HAPPY

From the desk of
Tobe Fit

Thanks for reading my book.
I hope you liked it.

Janey and I want to make sure that you all
get to go on your own "Fresh Adventures" so
we put a set of TICKETS in this book just for you!

Have fun making these snacks*
(with just a little help from a grown-up).
They're yummy and good for you too!

─ KIDS: ─

To download more copies of
"Tickets to FRESH Adventures"
and for more fun food activities,
visit us at:
www.foodplaykids.com

─ PARENTS and TEACHERS: ─

For more food and nutrition education resources
and to find out how to bring FOODPLAY's
national award-winning live theater shows
to your schools and special events,
check out:
www.foodplay.com

* Caution: Most of these snacks are not recommended for
children under age five due to possible choking risk.